The Tree
that Talks to Me

by Marjory Morrison

DORRANCE
PUBLISHING CO
EST. 1920
PITTSBURGH, PENNSYLVANIA 15238

Dorrance Publishing Co
585 Alpha Drive
Suite 103
Pittsburgh, PA 15238
Visit our website at www.dorrancebookstore.com

ISBN: 979-8-8860-4345-7
eISBN: 979-8-8860-4510-9

Acknowledgements:

I dedicate this book to all the children in the world, especially in this time of confusion and chaos. I want to give them hope and let them know that they have a safe place for their dreams and their voices to be heard.

I go into the forest once a day;
to talk to the tree that talks to me.
I call to him from the forest floor;
it takes him a while to answer me.
Then like a whisper of the wind,
I hear his voice welcoming me in.

We talk every day for weeks on end.
We share our thoughts, friend to friend.
I know this tree and he knows me.
He was already grown
when I was just a child.

He gives me shade when I try to hide
from the heat of the sun,
resting on the roots at the base of his trunk.
When I need to cry he comforts me,
inviting me into his branches and
gives me the courage to never give up.

I'm always amazed at how strong he is.
He is beautiful!
In my heart, I know that all my secrets
are safe with him.

On my way home from school one day,
I was tired. I was worried about not having my
homework ready that the teacher had asked for.
My teacher said, "What happened?
I've given you plenty of time!"
As I walked, I thought about
how to tell my secret to my friend.

I knew my secret was safe
with him and that I would have
no problem talking to him.
As I went to the forest
and called out to him,
as I always did.
I waited for his response,
suddenly I felt his branches
moving gently in the wind.
"Hello, my child,
sit on one of my branches
and talk to me a while.

"I am home for many
creatures great and small,
from caterpillars and butterflies,
to birds, squirrels, and raccoons.
They keep me company
while I provide shade
and clean the air you breathe.
To some, I look like
a big plant, but I have feelings too."

I tell myself, "Nothing can go wrong
with a friend like this".
On the days I feel weak,
I look forward to seeing my friend.
I find peace under his shade
and he gives me fresh air to breath.

As I was talking to Him one day,
I told him that I might not
be able to come during the rain,
but that my thoughts and heart
would be there with him.
I said, "I will see you tomorrow
if our Creator allows it".

Every day we spend time together
talking and listening to each other;
the forest listens too.

On the way home I decide to give him a name. Many ideas cross my mind on what to call my quiet friend; the name that he might answer to.

The Quiet Oak seems
like the best name.
I think he likes it.
That is settled, we both agree.
The Quiet Oak becomes his name.
He whispers in my ear,
"That will be the name
I will answer to".

It becomes a routine
that we see each other often.
We grow closer together
in friendship and his size grows too.

When Autumn comes, the Quiet Oak says to me,
"My leaves will turn a different color;
sometimes they will
be bright and sometimes not.

Please, don't worry,
even though my leaves
will fall off, I am still alive,
and my heart will be too.
Your secrets will be safe with me;
keep coming so I can watch you grow."

On one of those visits in early fall, as I was
standing at the trunk and touching his bark,
I ask what he sees at night and would He tell us all?

The Quiet Oak says that He had heard
and seen many things, both great and small.
Shooting stars, comets, cycles of the moon,
galaxies of stars, the sound of thunder
after a lighting strike,
and the beauty of the storm
in all it's dangerous forms.

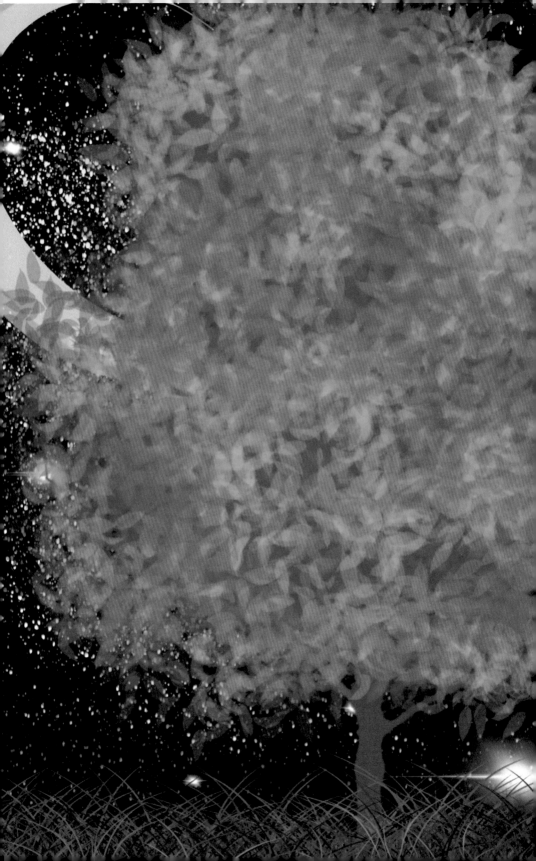

Then there are the animals
in these woods that rely on me.
The shelter I provide as home
and source of comfort to so many.
Animals birthing their young
to seeing them flying
from their nest for the first time.
I share this as
a good memory for you.
Come back tomorrow
if you have time and
I will tell you more
of everything I see.

Every day that passes,
we become closer as friends.
We share all our secrets;
nothing seems to be left unsaid.

It's winter now; my Quiet Oak friend sleeps.
He's soaking up the nutrients
that will help Him grow even more.
It's much too cold for me to walk outside.
I miss my friend. I hope he doesn't think
that I have forgotten him.

While at home, as I look through the window
of my bedroom I know that he is asleep.
I watch the moon for him.
I also see the dew that keeps the forest refreshed.
I look around and see all the forest asleep.
I will come back and tell my dear Quiet Oak friend,
what I saw when he was asleep.